THE

SHARK

DICTIONARY

For my little ones, Elena and Nathaniel
—S. G.

*For my husband, Quan, whose love and
support have been invaluable*
—L. L. T.

Acknowledgments

*The author and editors gratefully acknowledge the assistance
of John McCosker, Director of the Steinhart Aquarium, California
Academy of Sciences, San Francisco, as well as of John Gustafson.*
—S. G.

*Many thanks to Christine Benjamin and Lisa Hassur for their
help. I could not have done it without them. And a heartfelt
thank you to all the special women in my life.*
—L. L. T.

Published by Checkerboard Press, Inc.
30 Vesey Street, New York, NY 10007

EYE ON NATURE
THE SHARK DICTIONARY

Written by
Sarah Gustafson

Illustrated by
Laura L. Trang

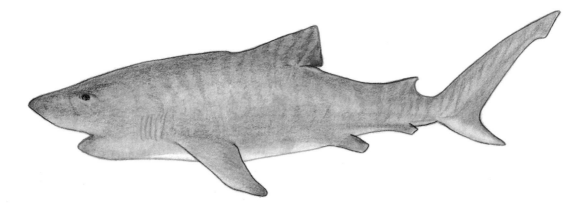

CHECKERBOARD PRESS

NEW YORK

WHAT MAKES A SHARK A SHARK?

In the mysterious realm of the ocean lurk some of the most fascinating creatures on Earth—sharks. Scientists have discovered that there are nearly 400 different kinds of these powerful animals, and they come in many shapes and sizes. They can be as tiny as the 6-inch-long dwarf shark or as huge as the 50-foot-long whale shark. They can be flat like the angel shark or torpedo-shaped like the mako. Sharks live in every ocean in the world—from the tropics to the poles and from coastal areas to the open ocean. Some live near the sunny surface of the water and others in the cold, dark depths. Some lay strange eggs called mermaid's purses, and others give birth to fully developed young.

But what makes a shark a shark and not just another fish? Like other fish, sharks spend all of their lives in the water. They use fins to swim and they breathe through gills. But they differ from other fish in important ways. First, the scales that cover a shark's body aren't the soft, delicate scales of other fish. Instead, they are hard, tiny teeth! Also, the skeletons of most fish are made of bones, whereas a shark's skeleton is made of cartilage—the same material that makes up the tip of your nose. Most sharks have extremely powerful jaws and sharp teeth.

In the movies, sharks are often shown as nothing more than eating machines, a menace to people. Although some sharks can be dangerous, they are fascinating animals that scientists are only beginning to understand. As you turn the pages of this book, you'll discover what makes sharks interesting and unusual creatures!

How to Use This Dictionary

Just like all dictionaries, **THE SHARK DICTIONARY** will tell you several things about the words in it. To get started, let's take a look at a definition of the word "shark."

entry word / spelling   *pronunciation*   *part of speech*   *definition*

shark
(SHARK) *noun*

A shark is a kind of **fish** that typically has a long, tapering body and a skeleton made of **cartilage**. Like all fish, sharks

breathe through a pair of **gills.** Unlike **bony fish**, however, sharks have at least five pairs of **gill slits**. Also, the scales that cover their bodies are actually tiny, sharp teeth called **denticles**. Some female sharks give birth to living young, while others lay **eggs**. Most sharks are **predators**.

Notice that in addition to the meaning, or *definition,* of the *entry word*, you also learn the correct *spelling* of the word as well as its *pronunciation*. The pronunciation tells you how to sound out the word. (See the *pronunciation key* at the front of this book.) Last, you learn the *part of speech* of the word you're looking at—a noun, verb, or adjective. Nouns are names of things, verbs are action words, and adjectives describe things.

    THE SHARK DICTIONARY also features words in bold within each definition. These are other entry words that can be looked up. For instance, on the "shark" definition above, you'll see there are several words in bold. If you wanted to find more information about "gills," "cartilage," or "predators," you'd know there are definitions on each of these within the dictionary.

    This book is all about sharks and how they live. Whenever you are reading or learning about sharks and come upon a word you don't know, look it up here. Or read **THE SHARK DICTIONARY** from beginning to end. You will discover a world of interesting facts about these fascinating fish!

angel shark
(AYN-jul SHARK) *noun*

An angel shark a is type of shark whose head and body are broader and flatter than those of most other sharks. An angel shark's **pectoral fins** are very wide and look a little like the wings of an angel. There are several kinds of angel sharks, and they all live on the ocean floor. They often bury themselves in sand or mud so they can ambush small **fish**. Sometimes angel sharks lie very still on the seafloor for several weeks. At other times they may travel several miles in just one night.

aquarium
(uh-KWAYR-ee-um) *noun*

An aquarium is a tank filled with water where **fish** and other **aquatic** animals may live. A public aquarium is a good place to see sharks. Some aquariums have special tanks called shark channels. These doughnut-shaped aquariums allow sharks to swim without stopping or having to turn around.

aquatic

(uh-KWAT-ik) *adjective*

Aquatic means living in the water. Like all **fish**, sharks are aquatic animals. Some aquatic animals live in lakes, rivers, or other bodies of fresh water (water that isn't salty). Others, called marine animals, spend their lives in the salty ocean. Still other animals move back and forth between fresh and salty water. Sharks are marine fish, although some, such as the **bull shark**, can survive in fresh water also.

The octopus, starfish, and seal are all aquatic animals.

basking shark

(BASS-king) *noun*

The basking shark is one of the biggest and most gentle sharks in the world. As it swims slowly along the surface of the water with its huge **mouth** wide open, the basking shark looks as if it's basking, or warming itself, in the sun. Actually, the **fish** is eating **plankton**, which it filters from the water with its long **gill rakers**. When plankton become scarce, this shark sheds its gill rakers and hibernates on the sea bottom.

batoid

(BAT-oyd) *noun*

A batoid is a type of **fish** that is closely related to sharks. Batoids include more than 500 kinds of skates and rays. Like sharks, their skeletons are made of **cartilage** and their bodies are covered with **denticles**. From above, however, most sharks look like long ovals, while batoids are shaped like circles or triangles. Their bodies are flattened like pancakes, and their winglike **pectoral fins** are big and broad. Most batoids live on the ocean bottom, where they feed on fish and other animals.

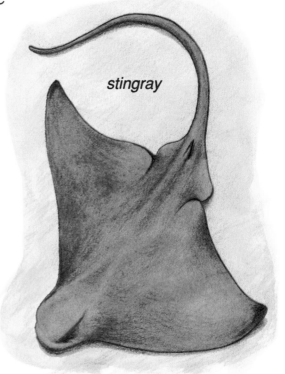

stingray

blue shark

(BLOO) *noun*

With its deep blue back and snow white belly, the blue shark is one of the most beautiful sharks living in the open ocean. Some blue sharks **migrate** as far as 2,000 miles every fall and spring. Their long **pectoral fins** help them to swim gracefully. Just like baby mammals, baby blue sharks develop inside their mother. Female blue sharks usually have between 40 and 50 **pups** in a single **litter**. Sometimes they can have more than 160!

bony fish
(BOH-nee FISH) *noun*

A bony fish is one whose skeleton is made of bones. There are more than 30,000 species of bony fish in the world. Sharks are not bony fish; their skeletons are made of **cartilage**. There are two other big differences between sharks and bony fish. A shark's skin is covered with **denticles**, which are **scales** that are actually teeth. By contrast, most bony fish have flat, overlapping **scales** covering their bodies. Also, a bony fish has only one opening on each side of its head that leads to its **gills**. A shark has between five and seven **gill slits** on either side of its head.

bony fish

shark

bull shark
(BULL) *noun*

The bull shark is a big shark that sometimes attacks humans. Bull sharks can live in salty or fresh water. In the United States, bull sharks live in the Mississippi River. They have been found as far upstream as Alton, Illinois, located more than 1,700 miles from the sea. While some bull sharks have survived more than five years at a time in fresh water, scientists have discovered that they return to the ocean to give birth.

cannibal
(KAN-uh-bul) *noun*

An animal that eats others of its own kind is a cannibal. Many sharks are cannibals. In fact, the most common **predators** of some sharks, aside from people, are other sharks. Once, a **tiger shark** was caught in the Gulf of Mexico with a **bull shark** in its belly. Inside the bull shark's belly was a blacktip shark, and inside the blacktip shark was a **dogfish shark**! Some sharks are cannibals even while growing inside their mother's body. A baby shark that is bigger than others in its **litter** will sometimes eat the smaller ones, and **eggs**, too.

whitetipped reef sharks

cartilage
(KART-ul-ij) *noun*

Cartilage is a type of body tissue that is softer than bone, yet tougher and more flexible. Unlike other **fish**, a shark doesn't have a bone in its body; instead, its skeleton is made of cartilage. Wiggle your ears and the end of your **nose**—they are made of cartilage, too. Under water, cartilage weighs only half as much as bone. Thus, having cartilage instead of bone helps sharks to float.

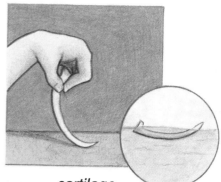

cartilage

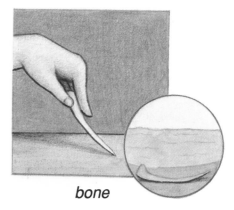

bone

catshark

(KAT-shark) *noun*

A catshark is a type of shark that lives in deep water and hunts for food along the seafloor. There are many kinds of catsharks, and they all have teeth like knife blades in their upper **jaws**. They use their sharp teeth to gouge **prey**. Like some four-legged cats, catsharks have colorful patterns of stripes and spots. Catsharks can grow to about three feet long. One kind of catshark can gulp enough water to swell up to nearly twice its normal size when it feels threatened.

The swell shark is a kind of catshark.

mermaid's purses

chum

(CHUM) *noun*

Chum is a mixture of things like whale oil and chunks of animal flesh and intestines. Fishermen use chum as bait to attract sharks.

circle

(SER-kul) *verb*

Circle is the word **ichthyologists** use to describe the way some sharks swim before attacking. In circling, the shark begins to swim slowly in a big circle around **prey**. Then it swims faster and faster in smaller and smaller circles, getting ever closer to its meal. While the shark is circling, it examines its prey and may even bump or nudge it. When the shark is ready to attack, it stops circling. It rushes straight at its victim, lifts its head up, opens its **mouth** wide, and bites.

bonnethead sharks

cookie-cutter shark

(KOOK-ee-KUT-er) *noun*

The cookie-cutter shark looks as if it has a saw stuck in its **mouth**. This foot-long shark's mouth is very wide and full of teeth. The teeth in its lower **jaw** are arranged in straight bands that go from side to side as well as from front to back. The cookie-cutter eats by taking ball-shaped bites out of **fish** and whales much bigger than itself. It may shed an entire row of teeth at a time. If the teeth fall out while the shark is eating, it may swallow them! Scientists sometimes find whole sets of teeth within the stomachs of cookie-cutter sharks.

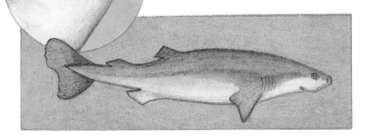

14

Dd

denticle
(DENT-ih-kul) *noun*

A denticle is one of the many small, hard **scales** that cover a shark's skin. Denticles are actually sharp teeth. In fact, they sometimes are called "skin teeth." Scientists believe the teeth in a shark's **mouth** probably evolved from denticles. About the size of a grain of sand, each denticle points towards the shark's tail. If you rub a shark in the opposite direction, the denticles will scrape your skin right off.

close-up of denticles

salmon shark

dorsal fin
(DOR-sul FIN) *noun*

The **fin** on the back of a **fish** is called a dorsal fin. Most sharks have two dorsal fins. The one in front is usually shaped like a triangle and is larger than the back one. When a shark swims close to the water's surface, this front dorsal fin may stick out of the water. Both dorsal fins help a shark to steer underwater and to keep from rolling side to side.

soup fin shark

15

dwarf shark

(DWORF) *noun*

The dwarf shark is the smallest shark in the world. Full-grown dwarf sharks are only five to six inches long—smaller than a banana! They live in very deep water near the ocean floor.

egg

(EGG) *noun*

An egg is the round or oval body laid by many female **fish**, reptiles, and other animals, and by all female birds. The egg is where a baby animal develops. Many sharks lay eggs, but they are different from the eggs of **bony fish**. Some bony fish lay millions of little round eggs each year, while sharks rarely produce more than 50 eggs in a year. Some sharks' eggshells are called **mermaid's purses**. They are tough and leathery and come in many interesting shapes. Not all sharks lay eggs. Some are **live-bearing sharks**, which means they give birth to fully developed babies.

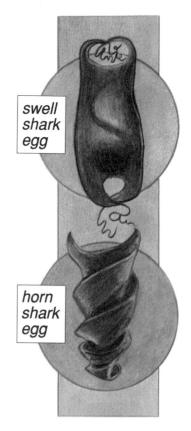

swell shark egg

horn shark egg

elasmobranch

(ih-LAZ-muh-brank) *noun*

Elasmobranch is the scientific name for the group of **fish** that includes sharks and their cousins, the **batoids**. The word *elasmobranch* means "plate gills." The **gills** of sharks and batoids are held up by thin plates of tissue inside their throats. The gills open to the sea through **gill slits**. All elasmobranchs have skeletons made of **cartilage**, and their bodies are covered with **denticles**. They also all have teeth, and old teeth are often replaced with new ones.

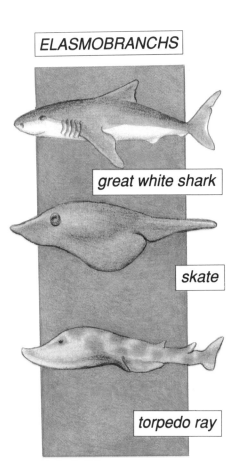

ELASMOBRANCHS

great white shark

skate

torpedo ray

electric field

(ih-LEK-trik FEELD) *noun*

An electric field is an invisible force field caused by electric charges. All animals produce weak electric fields around themselves. Using its **electroreceptor**, a shark can sense the electric fields of its **prey** from at least ten inches away.

The zebra shark can sense the electric field produced by the hermit crab.

electroreceptor
(ih-LEK-troh-ree-SEP-ter) *noun*

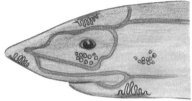

An electroreceptor is an organ
that a shark has that enables it
to detect the **electric fields** produced
by other animals. A shark's electroreceptor is in its head. Around the
shark's **nose** and **mouth** are
tiny holes, called pores. These
pores are openings for long tubes
that connect to other parts of the
electroreceptor. A shark can use its
electroreceptor to find **prey**—even
when it is hidden, such as a **fish** buried
in sand. The electroreceptor may also help
a shark find its way in the open sea.

*cross section
of snout, showing
the tubes and pores
of the electroreceptor*

endangered species
(en-DAYN-jerd SPEE-sheez) *noun*

An endangered species is any plant, animal, or other
organism that is in danger of becoming extinct, or dying out
completely. More than one hundred
kinds of sharks are threatened. Fished
for their meat, such sharks as the
thresher, **mako**, and **hammerhead**,
are being killed much faster than
they are born.

mako shark

feeding frenzy
(FEED-ing FREN-zee) *noun*

A feeding frenzy is a sudden and violent attack by a group of sharks upon **prey**. During a feeding frenzy, different kinds of sharks will swim to an area from all directions, attacking anything that moves or bleeds. They will even attack each other. Sharks behave more aggressively during a frenzy than when they are alone.

blue sharks

fin
(FIN) *noun*

A fin is a part of the body of a **fish** that sticks out like a wing or a paddle. Most fish have eight fins—a **pectoral fin** and a pelvic fin on each side, two **dorsal fins** on the back, an anal fin on the belly, and a **tail fin**. Fish use their fins to move, steer, and balance. The size and shape of fins differ from fish to fish.

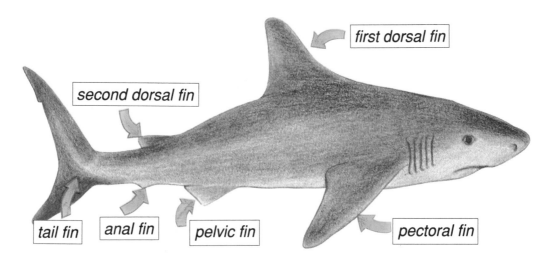

first dorsal fin

second dorsal fin

tail fin anal fin pelvic fin pectoral fin

fish

(FISH) *noun*

A fish is an animal with a backbone that lives in water all of its life, breathes through **gills**, has **scales** all over its body, and uses **fins** to swim. While most fish have bony skeletons (and so are called **bony fish**), sharks and other **elasmobranchs** have skeletons made of **cartilage**.

garibaldi (bony fish)

mako shark (elasmobranch)

frill shark

(FRILL) *noun*

A frill shark is a rare shark that lives in the deep sea. A frill shark has very long **gill slits**. They go all the way from one side of its head, under its neck, and to the other side. The skin around its gill slits grows outward in folds. This makes the shark look as though it is wearing a frilly collar. The frill shark is different from most other sharks in that its **mouth** is at the tip of its head, rather than on the underside. Frill sharks are thought to be very **primitive**. Many of their features are similar to those of sharks that lived millions of years ago.

gas bladder
(GASS BLAD-er) *noun*

A gas bladder is a sac filled with air, like a balloon (a bladder is a kind of sac, and air is a kind of gas). Most **bony fish** have a gas bladder inside their bodies near their stomachs. The air in the bladder keeps the fish from sinking. Sharks lack gas bladders, but they have developed other ways to keep from sinking. Many sharks have oil in their livers that helps them to float. Some must constantly move forward. Because a shark does not have a gas bladder, it can move straight up and down like a helicopter.

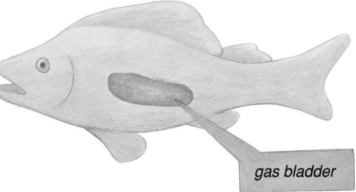

gas bladder

gill
(GILL) *noun*

A gill is an organ that provides oxygen to the bodies of many **aquatic** animals. All **fish**, including sharks, have two gills, one on each side of the head behind the **mouth**. To breathe, a shark brings water into its mouth, over its gills, and out through its **gill slits**. The gills take in oxygen from the water, just as a mammal's lungs take in oxygen from the air. Some sharks must move all the time in order to keep water flowing over their gills. If they stopped swimming, they would suffocate.

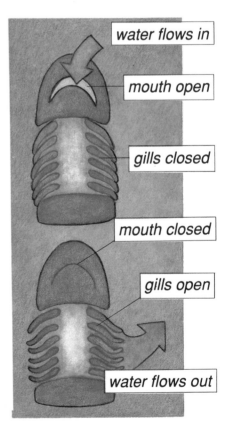

water flows in

mouth open

gills closed

mouth closed

gills open

water flows out

21

gill raker

(GILL RAYK-er) *noun*

A gill raker is the part of a shark's **gill** that keeps food from flowing out through the animal's **gill slits**. Gill rakers look like the bristles on a hairbrush. They stick out into the shark's **mouth**. Most sharks have short gill rakers, but **megamouths**, **basking sharks**, and **whale sharks** have very long ones. These sharks use the gill rakers to catch their food. When they open their mouths and swim forward, the gill rakers get clogged with **plankton**. The sharks then swallow the plankton and open their mouths for more.

long gill rakers

basking shark

whale shark

gill slit

(GILL SLIT) *noun*

A gill slit is a narrow opening in the skin covering the **gills** of a shark. Most sharks have five gill slits on each side of the head. A few types have six or seven pairs of gill slits. The slits are lined up next to each other like fence posts. Water flows in through a shark's **mouth**, over its gills, and out through the gill slits.

great white shark

(GRAYT WHYT) *noun*

The largest flesh-eating fish, the great white shark is one of the most dangerous **predators** in the world. Also called the "man-eater" shark, the great white attacks more people than any other shark. However, this huge fish usually eats marine mammals, often swallowing its **prey** whole. This shark can grow up to 21 feet long, weigh as much as 6,000 pounds, and have teeth three inches long.

hammerhead shark

(HAM-er-hed) *noun*

The unusual hammerhead shark has a wide, T-shaped head that looks like a hammer. The shark's eyes and nostrils are on the ends of each side of the hammer. The eyes of a big, 20-foot-long hammerhead may be 3 feet apart. Scientists know that hammerhead sharks often eat **stingrays**, because stingray spines are commonly found embedded in the hammerheads' **mouths** and **jaws**.

horn shark

(HORN) *noun*

The horn shark is a small shark that has spines that look like horns on its **dorsal fins**. It also has a blunt head. The scientific name for the horn shark means "different teeth," and this shark does have teeth that are different from most other sharks. It has sharp teeth in front for biting. In back are flat molars for crushing animals like sea urchins and clams to eat. A female horn shark's eggshell (called a **mermaid's purse**) is shaped like a screw so it will attach securely to the rocky crevice in which it is laid.

ichthyologist

(ik-thee-OL-uh-jist) *noun*

An ichthyologist is a person who studies fish. The word "ichthyologist" comes from the Greek word *ikthus*, meaning "fish." The study of fish is called "ichthyology." If you like to learn about fish, you could become an ichthyologist.

jaws
(JAWZ) *noun*

Jaws are the pair of bones that form an animal's **mouth** and hold its teeth. Sharks have short but very powerful jaws. In most sharks, the jaws are only loosely connected to the rest of the head. This allows a shark to open its mouth very wide and take big bites out of large **prey**. When a shark bites, it pierces its prey with the spiked teeth on its lower jaw. With the teeth on its upper jaw, the shark saws through its prey's flesh as it jerks its head from side to side.

whale

blue shark

lateral line
(LAT-uh-rul LYN) *noun*

A lateral line is made of rows of little holes along the head and side of a shark's body. These holes, called pores, help the shark to hear and feel movements in the water, like those caused by a fish or other prey. The pores open into sensory cells in the shark's skin. These cells send information about changes in the water to the shark's brain. Scientists believe a shark's lateral lines may enable it to detect an animal nearly 2,000 feet away.

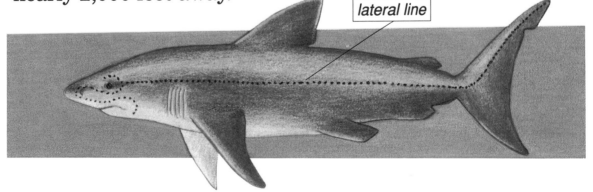

lateral line

lemon shark

(LEM-un) *noun*

The lemon shark is a medium- to large-sized shark with a wide, rounded **snout**. The lemon shark's two **dorsal fins** are the same size. This is unusual, since in most other sharks the front dorsal fin is bigger than the one in back. Lemon sharks are common in the shallow waters off the coast of Florida. They often rest on the seafloor while small fish pick parasites off them. Scientists know more about lemon sharks than most other types of sharks because they can survive in captivity

leopard shark

(LEP-erd) *noun*

The leopard shark is a grayish-yellow shark that has wide black spots on its back and sides, much like a leopard. Leopard sharks are considered harmless to humans. They grow to about five feet long, an average size for a shark. Leopard sharks are commonly found off the coast of California. Many people like to catch them for their meat.

litter
(LIT-er) *noun*

A litter is a group of sharks or other animals born of the same mother at one time. All of the sharks in a litter are sisters and brothers. Most **live-bearing sharks** have 6 to 12 **pups** in a litter. Some have more than 100 at a time.

live-bearing shark
(LYV-bayr-ing) *noun*

A live-bearing shark is one that gives birth to fully formed babies, just as mammals do. Instead of laying **eggs**, a live-bearing shark carries her developing young inside her body until they are ready to be born. Most sharks are live-bearing, particularly those that live in the open ocean. Their **pups** are bigger than the baby sharks that hatch from eggs. When a shark is giving birth, she does not feed. This may protect the newborn sharks from being eaten by their mother.

liver

(LIV-ur) *noun*

The liver is the large abdominal organ in many animals that helps to break down food. In many sharks, the liver also helps the animal float. These sharks have very large livers that are full of fats and oils. Because oil is lighter than water, it helps keep the sharks from sinking. (**Bony fish** have **gas bladders** to keep them buoyant instead of big, oily livers.) Sometimes sharks are killed for their livers. Shark liver oil is very valuable as a lubricant and as a base for paints.

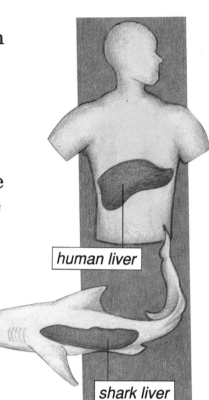

human liver

shark liver

Mm mako shark

(MAK-oh) *noun*

The mako shark is a dangerous shark with a sleek body and a pointed **snout**. Mako sharks can swim more than 20 miles an hour—faster than most other sharks. When caught on a fish hook, mako sharks often leap 20 feet into the air while trying to get away. This makes them a favorite of people who fish for sport.

28

megamouth

(MEG-uh-mowth) *noun*

As its name suggests, the megamouth is a large shark with an extremely big **mouth**. Inside its mouth are long **gill rakers** that strain **plankton** from the water. Scientists didn't know this shark existed until 1976, when one was accidently caught after it had swallowed a U.S. Navy ship's anchor near Hawaii. The megamouth lives in deep, dark water. It has tissue in its mouth that scientists think may glow in the dark. The shark might use this tissue to attract deep-sea shrimp and other small animals into the glowing cave of its mouth.

mermaid's purse

(MUR-maydz PURSS) *noun*

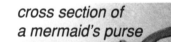

cross section of a mermaid's purse

A mermaid's purse is the capsule surrounding a shark's **egg**. Mermaid's purses are tough and leathery. Most are about the size and shape of a deck of cards. In addition, some have long tendrils that wrap around rocks and plants. The tendrils keep the egg safely in place until the shark hatches. The mermaid's purse of a **horn shark** is shaped like a screw. (See **catshark** illustration.)

migrate

(MY-grayt) *verb*

To migrate means to move from one area to another. Like whales, some kinds of sharks migrate hundreds of miles at various times of the year. They migrate to find food, to breed, or to give birth. While migrating, sharks tend to travel in groups made up of animals of the same sex and age. Sharks are very good navigators. They are able to find their way back to places they've been before after migrating many hundreds of miles through the open ocean.

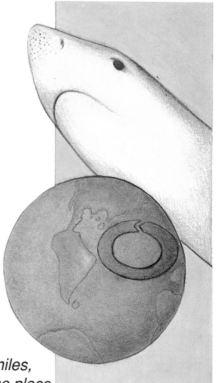

Even after migrating hundreds of miles, a shark is able to return to the same place.

mouth

(MOWTH) *noun*

The mouth is the part of the body that an animal uses for eating. In many **bony fish**, the mouth is at the tip of the head. On most sharks, however, the mouth is on the underside of the head. As a result, sharks are often described as "chinless." Having the mouth under the head gives a shark a very powerful bite, allowing it to cut large **prey** into small chunks.

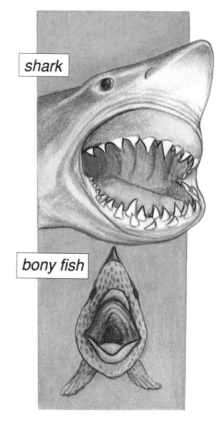

shark

bony fish

nocturnal

(nok-TERN-ul) *adjective*

The word nocturnal means active during the night. Most sharks are more active at night than during the day because they see best in dim light—that is, from dusk to dawn. At night, their pupils open wide. Sharks can also catch a lot of **prey** at this time since many of the animals they eat are also nocturnal.

during the day, pupils are tiny circles

at night, pupils are large circles

nose

(NOHZ) *noun*

The nose is the part of the body that an animal uses to smell. Sharks have such a good sense of smell that scientists sometimes refer to them as "living noses." They can smell blood in the water a half mile away! People use their noses for breathing as well as smelling. Sharks, however, use theirs only for smelling.

nostril

blood in the water

porbeagle

nurse shark

(NURSS) *noun*

The nurse shark is a sluggish shark that lives on the seafloor in warm, shallow waters. It has a short head with small eyes and a small **mouth**. A little flap of flesh called a barbel hangs down from each side of its mouth. It eats by first sucking such animals as shrimps, squids, and sea urchins into its mouth, then grabbing them with its small, sharp teeth. Nurse sharks can grow up to 12 feet long and weigh several hundred pounds.

pectoral fin

(PEK-tuh-rul) *noun*

A pectoral fin is one of a pair of **fins** just behind a fish's head. Most sharks have long, wide pectoral fins that act like the wings on an airplane to keep the shark from sinking. These fins also help the shark to balance, move up and down, turn quickly, and stop suddenly.

the pectoral fins of the great white

pilot fish

(PY-lut FISH) *noun*

A pilot fish is a type of **bony fish** that swims with sharks. There are several kinds of pilot fish. They usually swim in front of a shark's **snout** or beside its **pectoral fins**. These tiny fish gain a lot by swimming with sharks. After a shark kills its **prey**, the pilot fish can gobble up the scraps. Pilot fish are also protected by the shark, since none of their **predators** would dare come close enough to the shark to capture the pilot fish. By contrast, the shark doesn't gain anything from having the pilot fish around. It's not even interested in the pilot fish as food!

pilot fish swimming
with a thresher shark

plankton

(PLANK-tun) *noun*

Plankton are tiny **aquatic** plants and animals that float in large groups on the surface of oceans, lakes, and streams. Individual plankton are usually too small to be seen without a microscope, but thousands and thousands of them can tinge the water different colors. The three biggest types of sharks—**basking sharks**, **megamouths**, and **whale sharks**—eat almost nothing but plankton.

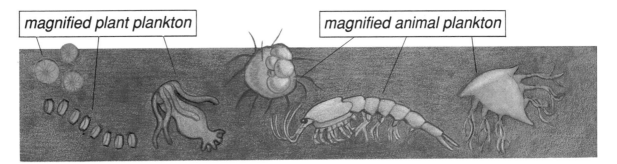

magnified plant plankton

magnified animal plankton

predator

(PRED-ut-ur) *noun*

A predator is an animal that kills and eats other animals. Many sharks are top-level predators, which means they aren't **prey** for any other wild animals. As top-level predators, sharks are important to the ocean environment. Without them, the animals they eat would overpopulate the ocean.

human

ANIMALS THAT HUNT SHARKS

dolphin

killer whale

ANIMALS THAT SHARKS HUNT

prey

(PRAY) *noun*

Prey is an animal that is killed and eaten by another animal. Fish, mollusks (such as squid and octopus), and crustaceans (such as shrimp and lobster) are prey for many sharks. Some sharks also eat seals, sea lions, and other marine mammals. Sharks in turn sometimes serve as prey for other animals. The most common predators of sharks are whales, other sharks, and people.

seal

fish

other shark

sea bird

34

primitive
(PRIM-ut-iv) *adjective*

The word primitive describes a plant, animal, or other organism that is at an early stage of evolution. Some people believe that sharks are primitive—that they haven't changed much in hundreds of millions of years. Actually, most sharks have evolved just like other animals have, even though some sharks still have some of the features their ancestors had. Sharks have swum the oceans for about 400 million years, and are among the Earth's oldest living creatures.

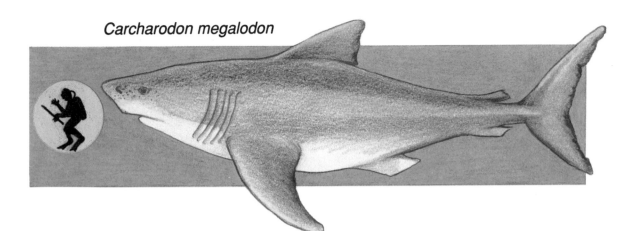

Carcharodon megalodon

propel
(pruh-PEL) *verb*

To propel means to make something move or stay in motion. A shark propels itself through the water by sweeping its powerful **tail fin** from side to side. Sharks normally drift or swim slowly with the current, but they can speed up very quickly when they need to. Some sharks can propel themselves to more than 20 miles per hour.

pup
(PUP) *noun*

A pup is a young shark. Shark pups are not taken care of by their parents. From the moment they are born they are on their own. Born with many sets of teeth, they are able to capture prey and defend themselves right away without any help from another shark.

baby swell shark leaving its mermaid's purse

remora
(rih-MOR-uh) *noun*

Like the **pilot fish**, the remora is a **bony fish** that is often found with sharks. The remora has an odd, disk-shaped **dorsal fin** that works like a suction cup. Using this fin to attach itself to a shark, the remora can hitch a ride as the shark swims. When the shark rests, the remora detaches itself, then picks off other, smaller animals living on the shark's body, **mouth**, and **gills**. In this way, the remora gets a meal and the shark gets cleaned! Remoras also attach themselves to sea turtles, whales, and other animals.

top view of a remora

a remora attaching itself to the underside of a lemon shark

scale

(SKAYL) *noun*

A scale is a thick piece of tough skin that protects a fish. Most fish have scales all over their bodies. The scales of **bony fish** are usually arranged like shingles on a roof, with the front end of each scale attached to the skin and the loose back end overlapping another scale. A shark has special scales, called **denticles**, that are very similar to its teeth. The top of one denticle fits into the groove of another.

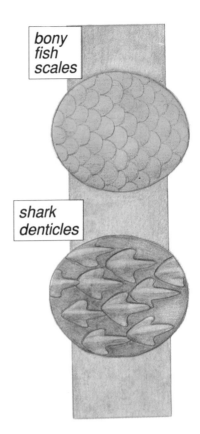

bony fish scales

shark denticles

school

(SKOOL) *noun*

A school is a large group of fish or other **aquatic** animals swimming together. Some types of sharks travel in schools. For instance, scalloped **hammerhead sharks** gather in groups of up to 100. By day, they swim close together and sometimes flash their white bellies at one another by rolling over and over. Scientists think the sharks go off on their own at night to hunt. **Spiny dogfish** also travel in schools. Each school is made up of either all males or all females.

hammerhead sharks

shark attack
(SHARK uh-TAK) *noun*

A shark attack is an assault on a person by a shark. Fewer than 100 people are attacked by sharks each year around the world. In fact, more people die from bee stings than from shark bites. In most situations, sharks are more likely to swim away than to attack. Some sharks attack because they feel threatened, not because they are hungry. When a shark is about to attack, it raises its **snout**, arches its back, and points its **pectoral fins** downward. Then it lunges forward with its **mouth** wide open.

great white shark

shark billy
(SHARK BIL-ee) *noun*

A shark billy is a stick that divers use to defend themselves from an attacking shark. The stick has a nail or other sharp object at the end of it. As the shark nears the diver, the diver hits the shark on the **snout** with the billy. This usually holds off the shark long enough for it to lose interest or for the person to get help.

great white shark

shark cage

(SHARK KAYJ) _noun_

Made of steel bars and mesh and about the size of an elevator car, a shark cage is used by divers to study and take pictures of sharks. A diver gets inside the cage while the cage is still on a boat. Then the cage is lowered into water where sharks are swimming. The cage protects the diver from **shark attacks**. A shark cage should probably be called a person cage, since the diver is inside the cage, not the shark!

shark meat

(SHARK MEET) _noun_

Shark meat is the term used for the flesh of a shark when it is eaten. Shark meat is tender and full of flavor. Many sharks are fished for their meat, including **mako sharks**, **thresher sharks**, and **spiny dogfish**. In fact, some sharks are threatened, which means that so many of them have been caught for food that they are in danger of becoming extinct. As one **ichthyologist** points out, "There are a great many more sharks eaten by people than there are people eaten by sharks."

thresher shark

sharkskin
(SHARK-skin) *noun*

Sharkskin is leather made from a shark's skin. It is used to make things like shoes, wallets, and belts. Sometimes sharkskin is made with the rough **denticles** left on. Then it can be used as sandpaper to smooth and polish wood and stone. In Japan, sharkskin with denticles was once used to wrap around sword handles to make the swords easier to grip.

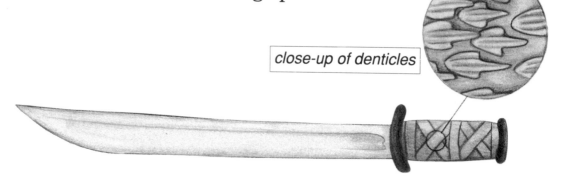

close-up of denticles

sixgill shark
(SIKSS-gill) *noun*

The sixgill shark is a deep-sea shark that has six pairs of **gill slits**. Scientists think the sixgill shark is probably more **primitive** than most other sharks, which have just five pairs of gill slits. Also, sixgill sharks have only one **dorsal fin**, and their upper **jaws** don't move around as much as those of other sharks. Sixgill sharks live as much as 6,000 feet under the sea and are among the greatest **predators** of the deep ocean.

snout
(SNOWT) *noun*

The snout is the part of an animal's face that sticks out in front and contains the **nose** and the **jaws**. Most sharks have long snouts, with nostrils on either side of the snout tip. The **mouths** of most sharks are on the underside of the snout beneath the eyes.

great white shark

spiny dogfish
(SPY-nee DOG-fish) *noun*

The spiny dogfish is a small, grey shark that has a sharp spine in front of each **dorsal fin**. The spiny dogfish uses these spines for defense. A **live-bearing shark**, the spiny dogfish develops inside its mother's body for 18 to 24 months—longer than any other **aquatic** animal. Spiny dogfish are very common in the cold waters of the North Atlantic and North Pacific.

stingray

(STING-ray) *noun*

The stingray is a kind of **batoid** that has a sharp spine at the base of its whiplike tail. This spine looks like a little saw, with sharp barbs on either side. Coated with venom, the spine is used to sting **predators** and **prey**. From the head to the tip of the tail, some stingrays can grow to five feet long and have stingers six inches long. The stingray is a favorite food of **hammerhead sharks** and **bull sharks**.

Tt tail fin

(TAYL FIN) *noun*

The tail fin is at the end of a fish's body. Most sharks have a lopsided tail fin. The upper part contains the end of the shark's backbone, so it is longer than the lower part and comes to a point at the end. (On most **bony fish**, the two parts of the tail fin are the same size, since the backbone ends where the tail begins.) A shark sweeps its tail fin from side to side to **propel** itself forward through the water. It also uses its tail fin to move up and down quickly.

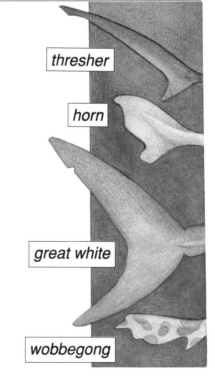

TAIL FINS OF VARIOUS SHARKS

thresher

horn

great white

wobbegong

thresher shark

(THRESH-ur) *noun*

A thresher shark is one whose **tail fin** is almost as long as the rest of its body. There are many kinds of thresher sharks, and they all swing, or "thresh," their long tails back and forth. By doing this, the sharks can herd fish into a tightly packed group so they're easier to catch. The sharks also use their strong tail fins to stun or kill their **prey**. Thresher sharks grow to 20 feet long and more than 1,000 pounds. They are often fished for their meat.

tiger shark

(TY-ger) *noun*

The large, dangerous tiger shark has stripes on its sides that resemble those of a tiger. They eat many things, from snails to dolphins, and sometimes even trash that has fallen into the water. They are more dangerous to humans than any other shark except the **great white shark**. These **live-bearing sharks** sometimes have more than 80 babies in a **litter**. Each baby is about the size of a full-grown house cat.

tooth

(TOOTH) *noun*

A tooth is the hard, bonelike structure that grows out of the **jaws** of many animals. A shark's teeth are set very loosely in skin, not rooted firmly in bone as your teeth are. As a result, shark teeth fall out easily, but there are always new ones ready to take the place of old ones. On some sharks, the entire set of teeth is replaced each week! The shape and size of a shark's teeth depend on what the shark eats. Meat-eating **great white sharks** have big teeth with razor-sharp edges. **Whale sharks**, which eat tiny plants and animals, have teeth smaller than a baby's fingernail.

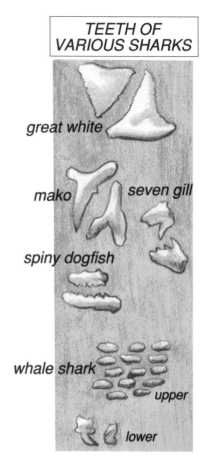

TEETH OF VARIOUS SHARKS

great white

mako

seven gill

spiny dogfish

whale shark

upper

lower

walking a shark

(WAW-king) *verb*

Walking a shark means to move a shark around underwater to help it breathe. Some sharks, such as **great white sharks** and **hammerheads**, must move constantly to keep water flowing over their **gills**. If they stopped swimming, they would die from lack of oxygen. Sometimes a shark living in an **aquarium** gets hurt and cannot swim. Then someone must "walk" it to keep it alive until it can move on its own again.

blue shark

whale shark

(WAYL) *noun*

The whale shark is the biggest **fish** in the world. Some whale sharks are 60 feet long and weigh 30,000 pounds. That's almost as long as a bowling lane and heavier than a double-decker bus! Their skin alone is four inches thick. These huge sharks eat tiny plants and animals and are not dangerous to humans. They have very small teeth and large **gill rakers**.

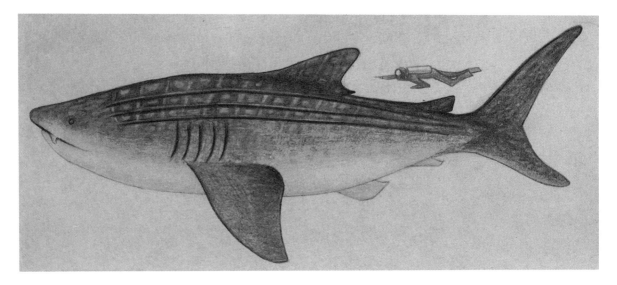

wobbegong

(WAH-bee-gong) *noun*

The wobbegong is a type of shark that lives on the seafloor and has a flatter body than most other sharks. A wobbegong shark is gray or brown, with lighter-colored blotches and spots all over its body. It has flaps of flesh growing out from its **mouth** that help it blend in with weed-covered rocks. Wobbegongs live off the coast of Australia.